“If we experience gratitude it will open up a realm of your life that previously you didn’t know existed.”

- Anonymous Nichiren Buddhist

30-DAY WORKBOOK TO IMPROVE YOUR LIFE AND OUTLOOK

ATTITUDE OF *Gratitude*

TOULA MAVRIDOU-MESSER

This edition of Attitude Of Gratitude 30-Day Workbook to Improve Your Life and Outlook first published in 2020 by 100 Percent Publishing.

ISBN: 9798580609508

This book is available at quantity discounts or bulk purchases. For information, please contact us at info@sultansofswag.com.

Disclaimer:

This book is not intended as a substitute for the medical advice of physicians or mental health professionals or any required treatment. The reader should regularly consult a physician or mental health professional in matters relating to his/her health, and particularly with respect to any symptoms that may require diagnosis, medical attention or therapy.

Although the author and publisher have made every effort to ensure that the information in this book was correct at the time of going to press, the author and publisher do not assume and hereby disclaim any liability to any party for any loss, damage or disruption caused by errors or omissions, whether such errors or omissions result from negligence, accident or any other cause.

Dedication

There's only one dedication that can truly be made and that's to all of the people and experiences that I have encountered during my life on this planet, thus far.

It always sounds a little corny to say that we are who we are because of what has happened to us, but of course it's the truth. It's the only truth.

It's also the truth to say that I am grateful for all of it, despite so much of it being very painful and difficult. Much of it I could have done without but those things happened, and I might as well benefit from them.

The incidents were survivable (even when I thought that they were not), and have taught me so much about myself and the inner strength that I am imbued with. A strength that developed exponentially and that I would never have known was there if it weren't for the trials and tribulations that got me to this point.

Whether who and what we encounter makes or breaks us, the implications are far-reaching and long-lasting. Opportunities for change and growth are always available to us and the power is within us to harness as and when we are ready to do so.

It might seem counter-intuitive to remedy many of the difficulties in our lives with gratitude and kindness but as you will soon find out, it works surprisingly well, is fast and is also abundant.

Remember that we also deserve to shower ourselves with gratitude and kindness too, and perhaps that's the best possible starting point for this journey on improving our lives and outlooks.

Thank you for joining me on this journey.

Contents

Join the #attitudetogratitude movement!

I'll start by saying how grateful I am that you have chosen my book "Attitude of Gratitude" to be your next read! Thank you!

I started my public gratitude journey by posting daily gratitudes on my social media quite some years ago, mainly as a way to focus my attention on the good things that were going on in my extremely stressful and difficult life.

Rather than letting the good things get swamped by the negative and then being overwhelmed by my circumstances, I found it really helped to sift through the day's events and pinpoint the things that were positive; the things that momentarily lifted my spirits and put a smile on my face despite feeling like I was carrying the weight of the world on my shoulders. There was always something to be thankful for however small and insignificant it had seemed at the time.

Soon those few things, once written down, added up to weeks and weeks of wonderful things; from easily finding parking spaces when and where I needed them, to getting a surprise 'gift' inadvertently included in my grocery delivery.

The best thing of all was that my daily gratitude had an uplifting effect on my friends too, some of whom also started looking for and sharing their daily gratitudes, which in turn inspired their friends to do the same. Here is a #dailygratitude that I posted on my personal page on August 18th, 2013.

"Grateful for that spark of energy that suddenly appears in your belly and spurs you on to take risks, to reach out to strangers, dream large and know that you are here to do something bigger and better than you have ever done before. Grateful for humility and honour.

Grateful that each day, each hour, each moment is a new beginning where we can stop doing one thing in favour of doing something new and changing our future in that split second. Grateful for infinite possibilities and opportunities. We can sit still all of our lives playing it safe only for the scariest things unimaginable to befall us or we can motivate ourselves and manoeuvre out of the way of boulders of others falling dreams and shards of disintegrating egos. This very moment is your life - live it!"

If you would like to be part of the #attitudeforgratitude community, sharing your daily gratitudes and positive moments with other like minded people, please come and join us here:

www.facebook.com/groups/AttitudeofGratitudeBooks

There will also be possibilities of having your own personal experiences and opinions anonymously included in future "Attitude of Gratitude" books, by filling out simple survey questions. Details of upcoming surveys will be posted in the group.

The Best Is Yet To Come!

Foreword

By Melanie Moore

The book you are holding in your hands has the power to radically change your life for the better in just 30 days. It has often been said that it takes 30 days to form a new habit – and what better habit is there to form than the daily practice of gratitude.

Eckhart Tolle put it quite simply; "If the only prayer you ever say in your entire life is thank you, it will be enough"

As a student and teacher of the Law of Attraction, I have long realised that gratitude is the secret sauce that marinates your manifestations – if you can maintain an attitude of gratitude while taking positive action steps towards your goal, your manifestations will happen sooner rather than later.

When you are in good health, have money in the bank and your relationships are rosy, it is easy to be grateful.

When you are having a good hair day, your children are doing their homework without being asked and the house is tidy and organised, gratitude is an easy emotion to access.

When you look in wonder at your newborn baby, when you are nestled in the delicious embrace of your lover, and when you see the sunset on a glistening ocean, you may even become overwhelmed with the immense sensation of gratitude.

Now for the plot twist. What about when your car breaks down at the most inconvenient time (not that there ever is a convenient time to break down)?

Or when you are in shock because you have received a worrying diagnosis, or you are crippled with anxiety because you don't know if you can pay the rent at the end of the month?

When you are left with the agony of a broken heart or are thrown a giant unexpected curveball by the Universe – gratitude is probably the furthest thing from your mind.

It is in moments like these you will find that gratitude is the fastest way to shift your vibration and to lift you out of despair.

Life will give you lemons and it will give you lemonade at various intervals, there are always gifts in the lemons – the lessons or "adversity" as Napoleon Hill puts it contain the "seed of equal opportunity." It is often your greatest trials that lead to your greatest triumphs.

I am deeply honoured that Toula asked me to write the foreword to her book – and I am so grateful that this task has served as a reminder of how powerful the practice of gratitude is.

Toula's wonderful book makes it easy for you to make gratitude a daily practice – the daily prompts and powerful questions will act as that special marinade for all your goals, dreams, and desires.

Magical things can happen in 30 days, so before you get started, set an intention for a wonderful outcome that you would like to have happen to you in the next 30 days, then hold that intention in mind every day while you complete the daily tasks.

To infinite possibilities, and in deep gratitude,

Melanie Moore
Big Vision Coach
www.melaniemoore.co.uk

Introduction

Last night I woke up with my heart pounding out of my chest. It had been a stressful day that ended with a surprise parking ticket.

We had set off early to go to Mum's care home - she has severe dementia/ Alzheimer's - to take her to a hospital appointment. The hospital appointment had been canceled. No one had told us and no letter had been sent. That pretty much set the tone for the rest of the day.

So, there I was wide awake in the dead of the night, drenched in a heavy cloud of doom, unable to get back to sleep and then panicking as I saw the minutes tick by knowing that I would have less and less time to sleep, if indeed sleep ever came.

All of a sudden, I realised that I had a trick up my sleeve that just might make all of the difference...and before I knew it I was once again in a deep slumber. That trick was simply expressing gratitude.

I told myself to start with 3 things that I could think of from yesterday to be grateful for.

It didn't actually take me very long to think of those 3 things: the weather was bright despite the winter chill, which gave us a chance to put on snuggly clothes, Mum is still able to come out with us for the day, which might not last too much longer and I had bought a gorgeous new sweater with a voucher I had been given ages ago and thankfully remembered was in my bag!

As I thought about those positive things I felt my heart rate slowing down and the gloom beginning to disperse, so I tried to think of 3 more things and then 3 more things and I can't remember what happened after that as I was fast asleep.

Gratitude is available to us all, whatever our circumstances and it works equally well for each and every one of us.

You don't have to be an 'expert,' highly educated, or even pious - gratitude doesn't care. Gratitude works for you whether you express it for the smallest of things or the biggest.

My entire life has always been full of drama and discomfort - I shall save the details for another time - but to give you an outline it started with me being placed into foster care at the tender age of just six weeks old and went downhill from there. However, I owe my sanity, my ability to keep putting one foot in front of the other, and the smile in my heart to gratitude.

Obviously, as a little girl, I had no idea of the concept of gratitude - I just knew that I was grateful for everything and said "thank you" continuously to the air in my bedroom, my dolls, my books - especially 'Beryl The Peril,' our loyal dog Patch and to myself. I was grateful for everything.

A few things that happen in life warrant the kind of gratitude that goes something like this, "Thank you for this for making me stronger!" or, "Thank you for this happening to me because I can deal with it!" I have said both of those a million times or more.

As a child, I knew that my life was different to most and that others didn't experience what I was experiencing but somehow, perhaps having read and re-read "What Katy Did," by Susan Coolidge numerous times, I had learned that being thankful really did make all of the difference.

Obviously I cannot guarantee that this book will magic away your difficulties and sleepless nights but I do know that being grateful and being kind fundamentally makes you a happier person and makes others happier to have you around, lifting everyone's spirits including yours. What could be better?

Gratitude is so simple and ultimately is an expression of love.
My love, hugs, and gratitude to you,

Toula x

Part One

Q. GRATITUDE: WHAT IS IT GOOD FOR?

A: Absolutely EVERYTHING!!

There are surveys and scientific data, too numerous to mention, that illustrate that just being grateful in your everyday life, for everyday things can fundamentally change everything in and about your life.

Just being grateful, it is said, can lift your spirits and change your mood, improve relationships, and make you more hopeful for the future. For those of us who sometimes feel down or anxious (and I am not talking clinical depression/ anxiety, serious mental illness, and serious health issues), just noticing the positive things about yourself, your life and what is going on around you can make all of the difference and in doing so increasing levels of:

- ◊ Energy
- ◊ Happy hormones
- ◊ Contentment
- ◊ Productivity
- ◊ Positivity
- ◊ Feelings of well-being
- ◊ Desire to eat well and live well
- ◊ Confidence
- ◊ Patience
- ◊ Taking notice of the little things and taking less for granted
- ◊ Awareness of other people's situations
- ◊ Kindness towards oneself and others
- ◊ Ambition
- ◊ Tolerance
- ◊ Encouragement
- ◊ Focus
- ◊ Hope
- ◊ Faith

There is so much material about gratitude and its benefits to mention but I wanted to find out the facts for myself for this workbook.

On the following pages are the results that I uncovered from my own 'gratitude' survey; real people talk about the many real benefits that they experience that come from regularly expressing gratitude.

Hopefully, seeing their results will encourage you to complete this simple 30-day gratitude workbook and immediately start seeing the benefits in your own life.

There's no magic formula for instantly increasing the positivity in your life but making a small effort every day to acknowledge the good in your life and the world around you will hopefully leave you feeling noticeably happier and more at ease.

In response to the question:

Do you or have you ever kept a gratitude journal or regularly and specifically expressed your gratitude?

This is how people replied:

"I have never kept a regular gratitude journal specifically, but I do keep a 'thought book', which is similar. In that book, I work with my son to dissect the things that didn't go well that day, (and what we could have done to change the outcome/prevent the rubbish thing from happening). The most important thing is that we then go on to acknowledge the good things that have happened that day and how they made us feel. I do pray gratitude though, rather than write it down. There are many things I'm thankful for and I think it's important to acknowledge them."

"I do it on and off. My sister is an alcoholic and we communicate our gratitude diaries. I started because she asked me to read hers daily to ensure that she actually did it."

"I always say thank you (even when not necessary!) and I try to be as humble as possible about my own 'luck.'"

In response to the question:

Do you think that expressing gratitude affected your physical health and how?

This is how people responded:

"Yes - whenever you are grateful for anything - you put more attention on it - what you have your attention on you get more of."

"Gave me energy!"

"I am a big believer in positive energy and approaching things in a mentally positive way. This has definitely helped me physically and daily gratitude, whether in written or conscious thought form, contributes to it."

"I think I am healthier because I start the day with a routine. After I write in the journal, I have breakfast and then move on to the daily tasks and then whatever I have planned for the day."

In response to the question:

Do you think that expressing gratitude affected your emotional health and how?

This is how people responded:

"It is easier to be calm and have faith in the present and future when I start the day with gratitude and see page after page (and a row of old journals) of praise and thanksgiving for the unending blessings and provisions of God. I am reminded that He has provided for me, amazingly and abundantly in difficult and easier times and He's not going to stop now."

"Yes. I think it did. It gave me a sense of the good things which were going on. Especially when it was hard to find something big to be grateful for as it made me focus on the little things. It made me look at the world more actively."

"It definitely helps with resolution of negativity and leaving things behind. I am also helped with the prayers of gratitude by reminding myself of how I have lots to be thankful for."

"I wasn't dwelling on the bad. I looked at the positive in my life and it made me feel better."

"Yes - by expressing my gratitude for the little things I seem happier all around. I notice more little wonders and that increases the gratitude. It is a snowball that just gets bigger and bigger by rolling."

"Positively it makes you feel polite, well mannered, lucky and grateful."

In response to the question:

Do you think that expressing gratitude affected your mental health and how?

This is how people responded:

"It made me realise how often I awfullise (sic) things and how easy it is to talk yourself into a negative state of mind."

"Yes, I was no longer focussing on the negative so my sadness and anger went away significantly."

"My focus has shifted from my feelings to really looking at my whole life from the small to the big stuff."

"Thinking in more detail about gratitude is particularly good to make you appreciate things you normally wouldn't and see that small things that are actually more important than bigger things."

"Felt happier and had more tolerance and patience."

In response to the question:

Do you think that expressing gratitude affected your mood stability and how?

This is how people responded:

"Yes, helps put things in perspective, it can lift darker moods."

"Not sure. My mood changes quickly, but it may help with calmness, slowing down to write."

"Gratitude makes you more mindful so always good for mood stability."

"Yes - I am calmer when I am grateful because I am happier and that affects how I deal with stress. I approach it in a rational manner as opposed to frantic which only increases stress."

"Yes. Happier."

In response to the question:

Do you think that expressing gratitude affected your stress levels and how?

This is what people said:

"Yes, coped better and stopped sweating the small stuff."

"Yes! It eased up my stress level much! Yes, I have a ton of homework, but I get to be in grad school and learn what I love!"

"Since I was focusing on the good, I wasn't stressing over things as much."

"Improves stress, due to lower anxiety."

"I think it makes me constantly re-evaluate the positives and this helps me to let go of negative thoughts and mood."

In response to the question:

Do you think that expressing gratitude affected your energy levels and how?

This is how people answered:

"Well, I sleep better at night when I am not fearful or worried about the future, because I remember God's goodness. Following a good night's sleep with my daily prayer routine, with breakfast and peace and a purposeful plan for the day, gives me more rest and therefore more energy for the day."

"Being happier led to me having more energy to do more!"

"Yes definitely improved energy, I had a real boost to enjoy the people around me and be more present."

"Possibly. My journal seems to develop into a list of goals. It's nice to check them off!"

"Yes because I seem more alive when I am doing gratitude posts. There are less dull periods because I can just look around and find another wee thing that I am grateful for in my surroundings."

"This one is hard. There were a lot of things trying to take away my energy, but at least I was upbeat when I was tired!"

In response to the question:

Do you think that expressing gratitude affected your being emotionally available to others and how?

This is how people replied:

"Well if you are grateful for the others in your life you tend to be more patient and available for them."

"Yes, through more patience and empathy."

"It made me more open to others! When you are thankful for PEOPLE, you don't judge them as much."

"I could not be as encouraging and available to others if I was bothered by my own concerns, ambitions and fears."

"I believe I am more tolerant and accepting of others' issues and I have more mental and emotional room because "my house is in order" to have room for helping others."

"I was able to see things from a different perspective and offer different advice and help."

In response to the question:

Do you think that expressing gratitude affected your ability to attain set goals and how?

This is what people said:

"Yes. My journaling tends to turn into a list of goals or a list of things that I want to accomplish."

"If you are grateful for every step along the journey it becomes an attraction point for the next."

"Yes, I managed to focus on projects and see them through to the end!"

"Goal setting was an important part of it for me. Doing the diary enabled me to reflect on my goals and how easy/hard they were to achieve. My sister's diary reflected her big goal of remaining alcohol-free and she found the diary helpful as she did not want to fail publicly."

"I would focus on how to make things better and realized my goals were important. Since I was happier I was able to focus on myself more."

In response to the question:

Please list any other benefits that you noticed that you feel came as a result of expressing gratitude.

This is how people responded:

"Awareness of all the things in life that I take for granted."

"I am more AWARE of the gifts of God and the kindness of other people. It makes me more observant. Being aware of the kindness of others makes me careful to thank them, which makes them happy. It's always good to make other people feel good."

"Calmer."

"I feel like I was more positive and upbeat, even when I was tired or ill from a cold or something. Because when you're sick, you are still grateful for a day of rest right when you need it!"

"One benefit was learning to share with other people."

"Sharing the gratitude posts has helped others around me who read them and have come to look for the next one. It affects how I first meet people - with more of a smile when I am in the gratitude zone."

"More loving and accepting to myself and others."

"Saying thank you to others (in a sincere way rather than a polite way) is absolutely uplifting for yourself and the person receiving your gratitude."

"Realising the power of saying 'Thank You' really opens you up to experiencing more joy."

In response to the question:

Please share any specific ‘gratitude’ anecdotes.

This is how people responded:

"I love greeting cards and I'm always buying funny/cute ones for friends and family members - it's a great way to let them know that you're thinking about them and appreciate their friendship even when you're not there to tell them in person. I love receiving them too!"

"We have been homeless (briefly) or on the edge of stability many times in our married life (32 years), but my prayer journal reminds me that God has never failed us. We have lived in 22 rental houses, and every one of them has been in a beautiful place with many blessings. I continue to give thanks for his provision, even as I wait for it, because my prayer journal has recorded his faithful and awesome provision."

In response to the question:

Please share details of changes within your personal relationships since expressing gratitude.

This is what people said:

"I'm actually a bit less tolerant of people who whine and complain about unimportant things!"

"Difficult marriage. Expressing daily gratitude to God keeps me mindful that even if humans fail me, God never will. Humans are fallible - God is eternal and faithful. I am not dependent on human relationships and provision. They are a blessing because they are a gift from God, whether in an easy or difficult state, and my hope is in Him. Not human beings. That frees me from an unhealthy emotional dependence on my husband or anyone else. God is my rock. My husband - and definitely I - are just mortals muddling along."

"When you are grateful for the conflicts that occur that point you in a better direction of relating to others, you learn from the conflicts."

"Much kinder and less critical than I was."

"I find when I am in the gratitude zone I am more of a listener when I am with my friends. This pause is welcome from my side and I really get to hear their details. Most times we are jockeying for position to tell our side when we have casual conversations with friends."

"When I am in a good mood, my husband and daughter are typically in good moods, too. If they are in a bad mood, I try and pull them up; if I am in a bad mood, they somehow pull ME up!"

"I think my friendships have changed, I feel I have found some enlightenment and I have removed any negative friendships from my life. I have learnt not to feel blame towards those who have hurt me in my life, but I turn it around and remember the positives. I am grateful for all that has happened in my life because it makes me who I am today."

"Just better."

In response to the question:

Please share details of what changes you think occur when you stop expressing gratitude and why.

This is what people said:

"Negativity begins to creep in if you're not careful."

"When you stop you fail to reflect."

"When I stop giving thanks and praise, I easily slip into a self-centered focus. I start a cycle of unconscious pride and self-entitlement, grumbling when I feel affronted or let down or unappreciated or if I am getting what I want or need. I start taking credit for the good things in life, which usually leads to depression when I fail to achieve or maintain them. I become fearful. Those things are actually results of forgetting God's goodness, not the results of failing to write it down regularly, but the consistent, daily recording of my blessings is what keeps me mindful. It's easy for me to slip out of that peace and confidence in Him when I don't keep the gratitude journal. I'm old. I forget easily."

"I become moody and negative until somebody reminds me to "look up" (aka look toward God instead of self!)."

"Stress creeps back in and my ability to deal with it positively is lessened. I want chips and fries more often. I believe our minds are complicated and it is a struggle between the negative and positive. Gratitude enhances the positive and pushes the negative away. The things that are bad for us come swooping back when we stop expressing our gratitude."

"Mood drops, energy levels drop, I guess because I'm focusing more on the things I think are wrong with my life."

"You are less mindful, less joyful and life can seem arduous."

"I think once you start it's hard to stop but as soon as I feel stuck, I do start doing daily thank yous to the universe for literally everything I experience in the day."

In response to the question:

What are you most grateful for at this very moment?

This is how people responded:

"Agnes Obel! Her songs speak the words I can't find myself."

"The sound of my grandson's high pitched communication!"

"I'm fasting and it actually feels good."

"That I have been drinking very good wine and that the air outside is fresh and that the night will be quiet and that there is a barn owl and a bat outside."

"My sister, Ruby."

"I am grateful that I don't have to live in a tent. I saw a lot of homeless people lining the edge of Angel Stadium."

"That I have a day to rest after a very hard job."

"Peace (I'm hiding in the bathroom!)."

"That in this moment all of my needs are met."

"My new rescue cat."

"Clarity."

In response to the question:

How easy is it for you to express your gratitude -

a) in person and b) in writing?

If you find one is easier than the other,
please explain why you think that is?

This is how people responded:

"I mostly do face to face as I like the immediacy of it. That being said, as a person challenged with dyslexia I'm not a massive fan of writing, although I do think there is something to sitting and taking time to jot down one's thoughts."

"In writing. When I write it's like I suddenly have a vocabulary that is hidden when I speak in person."

"Usually either way, unless circumstances test my stupid ego - like I'm grateful because someone called me on my bullshit and prevented me from shooting myself or someone else in the foot."

"In writing, because I'm better with my words that way and I get choked up in serious conversations face to face."

"It is easier in writing because I can add pictures and smiley faces or hearts."

"I find it easy to express gratitude, mostly to my immediate family - but easier in writing to my parents - not sure why that is."

"Both are easy, however writing an email or note is practical and an additional form of showing gratitude if someone has done something special for you. It's polite and gracious."

"Writing because I'm not very good at emotions in person."

"In person so that I can see the person's reaction."

"I like to express gratitude to people in person but like to journal my personal gratitude to life in writing."

In response to the question:

What are you most grateful for on a regular basis?
Something material or something spiritual/abstract?
Please give examples.

This is how people responded:

"My sister! My sister is my best friend and we have everything in common and I feel like I am a better person for having her in my life/knowing her."

"I am grateful that life has afforded me a small degree of independence which allows me to do things for others. I have a good job and own my own home. This has allowed me to help my sister and her husband through difficult times."

"The beauty of the land around me, the peace of my home, the love of my husband, the wonder of my grandson, the grace of his mother, the 'conversations' with heaven, sleep."

"I think very happy thoughts about my nieces. Those little girls make me very happy. I'm also happy that I am financially stable...not rolling in it or able to travel like I want, but my situation is stable."

"My kids turning out to be good people, my family that is always there for me, my job because after 15+ years of hating my job, I found one that I love."

"The Arts. They save my sanity and I see their importance, specifically film and music, also my sister, people who express themselves freely and honestly but watching how they affect others, say, not going out of their way to be rude but not holding back with honesty."

"My wife. My daughters. Health. Job. Writing. Yoga. Meditation. Dharma. The teaching and example of wise, creative, and courageous people. Beer."

"I am grateful that I have made my own path in life and not listened to others, it has given me strength and purpose to help others and that in turn makes me very happy."

"My curtains. So I can shut them."

"Spirituality. For my sense that I am connected."

"Being loved."

"To me something spiritual comes first, material comes second. I believe when your being is in touch with the universe, material things follow."

"Life itself."

In response to the question:

What might affect your attitude towards expressing your gratitude?

I.e. is it easier for you to be grateful for the little things when you are happy, or perhaps when life doesn't seem to be going your way?
Please give examples.

This is how people responded:

"When I'm low, it affects my ability to see the things I am grateful for, but when I focus on it, I notice them: nature, people, films, books. I think when I'm low, the things that I'm most grateful for are the things that make me feel less alone. I.e. people who think the same way/ artists who express the same kind of feelings and outlooks."

"When things aren't going well, I find it difficult to focus on the good things."

"Easier when I am happy but even more important when I am not."

"It's definitely easier to express gratitude when little things make you happy. When life isn't going your way, it is easy to start seeing only the bad side of everything and missing all the little things that could be making you happy."

"If I'm in a shit mood, you can hand me a million dollars and I might piss on it. So, the trick is to recognize when I'm in a shit mood. Usually stepping away and breathing helps. Or sometimes, just saying "Thank you" when things really suck helps in a perverse way."

"Grateful for little things when life is tough, like my two cats and my friends and family. My bed and Netflix lol."

"Perhaps jealousy may affect my ability to show gratitude...for example, if I was doing well at work but someone did better, I might feel hard done by or jealous and therefore not able to fully appreciate and be grateful for my own good work."

"Life has given me a share of unhappiness through my 70 years, but I have learned that when things don't go your way you should be grateful for the little things that make you happy!! Even if it's a beautiful flower, a small bird, a beautiful landscape, we should always be grateful to be alive."

"It's easier to express gratitude when you are on top of the world, though it might come in handy more when you are down in the dumps - either way gratitude is the crack that allows transcendence to higher states of vibration."

"It is always hard to find and express gratitude when depressed but reading my gratitude journal reminds me of the things that I can be grateful for."

"When I'm feeling down I find it difficult to show gratitude, but know it is what will pull me up."

In response to the question:

When you experience/witness someone being ungrateful, how does that affect you? Please give examples.

This is how people responded:

"It's very stressful. The times I've experienced people being ungrateful, they tend to be very unhappy in themselves and are unable to see the good in the little things, which is very sad."

"Frustrating. Infuriating when my girls don't show gratitude for what they have/are given, I am cross with them for 'acting spoiled.'"

"Makes me angry and upset."

"I can't explain why exactly but there is something that is 'killed' by ingratitude - an energy that just stops running. I think it has something to do with the fact that there is both a vast difference and a fine line between the operation of giving and receiving, (which is life-affirming and generative) and that of sacrifice and its exploitation (a vampiric contract which destroys the giver while it dehumanises the abuser). Ingratitude stands at the centre of the vampiric operation and that is why I think ingratitude shuts down generosity like someone putting the lights out; we are repelled by vampirism even when we are not its object and when we are its object shutting down is a matter of self-preservation. The same might be true about the way the universe/ God/ Heaven works: ingratitude surely shuts down the giving energy of the universe?"

"It's none of my business how other people behave."

"It jars because I know I wouldn't want to be treated that way. If it's directed at me I feel a physical hurt, as if I don't matter to the inflictor."

"Makes me feel sad and angry as they really don't know what they are missing out on. God, Angels, and the Universe love when you are grateful!"

"I cry. Seeing ungrateful behavior forces me to hold back tears. Also, it creates a feeling of not wanting to ever do anything for that person again."

In response to the question:

In your experience, does expressing your gratitude regularly appear to increase your good fortune? Please give examples.

This is how people responded:

"Yes, in a way. If you make the people around you know you appreciate them, they in return, seem to seek your company more."

"I think it does because it makes you happy and able to see good fortune easier."

"100% but I never do it for that. I believe in KARMA but I also believe we are all connected. Race, gender, social class do not matter. Many strangers have done great things for me and my family, people who did not know us at all. It was very moving. Happened a few times when I was in my teens. They were lessons. Otherwise, we would have ended up homeless and in danger. Germans in Germany came through for my family, especially my teachers. Found us home, furniture. We were stranded/stuck in Germany, after leaving Iran fearing for our lives...after the 1979 Islamic revolution. So in 1983/1984, my dad sent us out of the country (my mom, my sister and I). Teachers have played a big role in my life. From my teachers in Iran to Germany and in the U.S."

"I don't look at it that way. Or, well, sort of. I take great stock in the ability to see opportunity and feel gratitude. When I practice that I feel pretty flush."

"Yes - what goes around comes around I believe." "Not particularly but I'm superstitious so I try to express it anyway just in case the Universe thinks I'm being an arse."

"I think it increases what people are willing to help you with. Nobody wants to deal with someone who doesn't appreciate anything."

"About 6 years ago I stopped keeping a journal/ diary in the way I always had. I started writing three things I am grateful for in the morning and thinking of things I'm grateful for in the eve before sleep. That, in combination with meditation has changed my life so much for the better that I cannot really describe it. It is like being reborn. I still have struggles and depression but I have been able to poke my head through the veil of sorrow I was shrouded in my whole life."

"I'm not sure if I can say that this has definitely happened. When I feel more positive in my mood, things do seem to come to me though."

"It only increases my own awareness and acceptance of the things in my life."

"Yes, without a doubt but mainly because expressing gratitude changes my perspective and persona."

In response to the question:

Please describe a time when you were most overcome with gratitude. Please give examples.

This is how people responded:

"Just the other day, my sister was out and I messaged her saying I didn't feel well and she rushed home instantly and appeared at my bedroom door, out of breath asking what was wrong. While I felt an amount of guilt because I interrupted her day and made her worry, I am eternally grateful to have her there for me!"

"When my husband broke his leg and my friends rallied round to help, support, care and just be there for us. It made me question how I would've reacted in similar circumstances and if would do the same."

"When my partner's kids wrote me a letter to say that they liked me and it was all right to go out with their dad."

"When I moved into our new house, the exact 'wish list' my husband and I had each expressed having been met: way below market value so that we could afford it and sited in a place where the natural and spiritual energies make it feel like living in a prayer. Co-equal: when I was told that my grandson, who had gone into foetal distress and was delivered blue and unresponsive, was breathing, pink and healthy and out of danger."

"My friends David and MC surprised me with a card, cake, and gift a week before my birthday because they thought they wouldn't see me on my birthday, and then when I asked if I could come back on my birthday they said of course, you can never wear out your welcome here. It was wonderful."

"After having each of my kids, my friends and family were so incredibly helpful I would not have been able to do it without them. Also, there was a time my husband was really sick and in the hospital and the help I received (even in the form of a hot meal some nights when I got home from the hospital) was amazing."

"Standing in the kitchen with my wife, watching my girls running around with dresses and swim goggles on."

"When I lost my job: hearing how many people who worked for my company from the receptionist to some board members wanted to console and help me, and tell me how great I was at my job and tried to fight to keep me, that blew me away."

"I am always grateful to have a child as I didn't think I would.""When my coworkers and friends helped raise money for me to make multiple trips home to see my father in the hospital when he was hurt. Even strangers at work chipped in."

"When my car broke down in the turning lane. A man pushed me to get off the road so I wasn't blocking people anymore and I could call for a tow truck."

"A long time ago, when my Dad came to fetch me from university when I thought my heart and soul were broken."

"A friend I haven't seen or spoken to much for 10 years heard I was having a hard time after Fae was born, so she started writing to me every day to check on me and one day out of the blue she sent me a small surprise gift (a Neom organic perfume) just to make me happy."

"When my father died and a total stranger on a train comforted me when I cried."

"When my best friend presented me with a large cheque that I was not expecting at all!"

"In all honesty this is where I am now. I'm so happy I have so many amazing people in my life, my business has taken an amazing turn recently and I'm just in such a blessed place. That's not to say everything is perfect because it's not at all. I'm just feeling very happy content and at peace."

"On a recent trip to the Atlas Mountains, I was incredibly grateful to have had the opportunity to experience the people, culture and nature."

"Just yesterday. I just thought to myself (while driving) I am so happy. I am truly happy for the first time in my life. It's nice to have a partner in life and I am finally no longer alone in my journey."

In response to the question:

Do you think expressing gratitude is in any way connected with having spiritual beliefs? If yes, how? Please give examples.

This is how people responded:

"Slightly, but not exclusively. Spirituality seems to make some other people's lives better via them focusing on what they're grateful for. For me, no. Gratitude is owed to the things/people who make you feel grateful only. Though, when I've wanted something that I feel is out of my control, like to pass an exam, I find myself asking 'some higher power' to let me pass, and if I get what I wanted, I thank it. I think this 'higher power', for me, is passed relatives like my Uncle Jim."

"No. I think you can be grateful irrespective of beliefs. However, the manner by which you express gratitude could be hugely affected by your beliefs. I would imagine spiritualists to be more forthcoming and verbose in their gratitude."

"I don't think you need to have spiritual beliefs to express gratitude."

"I think gratitude is a spiritual belief. Ever read that book, The Slave, by Isaac Bashevis Singer? A Jewish slave wakes up every morning and says "I thank you.""

"Hmm not sure. I believe in treating others as we would hope to be treated/ paying it forward but not sure if that is classed as spiritual."

"It is for me because I am part of a spiritual process where gratitude is very important."

"Yep, I think I am quite spiritual. I love all that - I love the white feathers and thinking that loved ones can contact you or give you comfort when you need it."

"No, I think it shows respect towards another person."

In response to the question:

Do you think people who regularly express their gratitude take more personal responsibility for their own lives and happiness? Please give examples.

This is how people responded:

"I think so, yes. For me, life is a gift not to be wasted. So this means for me I have a responsibility to live a full life with happiness along the way."

"Yeah. It's true for me. When I'm in one of my "piss on a million bucks" moods, I tend to be more passive and bitter - a victim. When I'm grateful, I get off my ass and tend my own garden and take chances."

"Yes. I think those people are paying attention to things around them more."

"Yes. Because gratitude must be self-motivated; it requires one to have a shift in perspective and perception. It greases the cogs of one's personal Universe... thus allowing more to easily flow in and out."

"I think to take responsibility for your life you have to express gratitude for every aspect of life, the highs and lows, things you do well and mistakes you make. Responsibility also comes with personal growth as well as acknowledging and accepting every aspect of life."

In response to the question:

Please finish this sentence.
"My definition of gratitude is..."

This is how people responded:

"Being thankful for life and all the opportunities that it offers."

"Feeling grateful for the kindness, help and good fortune that comes my way."

"The awareness of grace and the grace of awareness."

"Being truly thankful for any kindness or gift bestowed upon you."

"Appreciating everything life has to offer, which is pretty amazing! Making sure I take the time to smile and acknowledge kindness, always try to give without expecting anything in return."

"Love."

"Being thankful for the people and things that enrich my life."

"To be in the present moment and know that in this present moment everything is ok."

"The excitement of needing to thank you 100 times and hug you NOW!"
"Respecting what you were given."

"Being happy with all aspects of your life and being at peace with yourself and your life."

"Being fully aware of the grace, abundance and the divine opportunities that surround. That I am vibrating at the level of Source - and my whole focus is on what I have and what I want more of."

"The selfless expression of the delight in life."

"Being thankful for everything that you receive in life each and every day no matter how large or small."

In response to the question:

Are humans the only creatures on Earth to feel and express gratitude? Please give examples.

This is how people responded:

"Of course not. Animals have feelings just like humans and probably show more gratitude than some humans. When dogs wag their tails at food time and when they know they are going for a walk that shows gratitude."

"No I think it is often seen in pets that they show gratitude, especially when you return home after a long day - their greeting always seems like an expression of gratitude for caring for them and returning to them (even if it is just to provide them with food and a bit of company!)."

"No way! My dogs are grateful to see all three of us every time! They wag their tails and jump all over us."

"No. Animals also feel gratitude from our love and care. Their behaviour is reflected by how they are looked after by their owners."

"When my cat had a hurt paw she held it up for me to see and deal with. Normally a shy and standoffish creature she curled up against me that evening and purred. A rare occurrence which I took to mean she was grateful for the removal of the thorn."

In response to the question:

Please share any other thoughts you may have about gratitude.

This is what people had to say:

"It's probably one of the fundamental life skills I'm teaching my sons."

"I need to express it more outwardly! I tend to think about it more to myself rather than share with those I care about."

"Whatever you put your attention on you get more of, so putting your attention on Gratitude gives you more to be grateful for - perpetual cycle."

"I think people who have gratitude, are generally better people, they find more happiness and peace with life and in turn life is more joyful."

"It's important to give perspective on life. It's easy to get wrapped up in the stresses and problems that are just everyday things and give them a huge amount of power. Gratitude gives a very important balance to the negatives in life."

"The ability to thank the Universe for every person, experience and emotion makes a very special person."

Part Two

It really is amazing what expressing gratitude can do for you. Now that you have read through all of these real-life responses, it's your turn and it's really simple.

Each day for the next 30 days you are going to form a habit that will help you to improve your life and outlook just by doing these simple things:

- ◊ Express gratitude
- ◊ Noticing what you usually take for granted
- ◊ Be positive
- ◊ Practise anonymous acts of kindness
- ◊ Stop and smell the roses

Just look at these examples of how to fill in your workbook each day for the next 30 days.

EXAMPLES:

Today I am grateful for:

Rain: it gave me a chance to slow down and reflect on life/ food in the freezer: I can save time and money by not going to the store in the rain today/ reminder from the dentist: I totally forgot to make an appointment for my annual check-up.

Today I took these things for granted:

I woke up this morning healthy and rested/ my car enabled me to get to work safely and dry, whilst listening to the radio in comfort/ the immense work and creativity that goes into creating a television show for my enjoyment.

Today I experienced these difficulties that I improved upon with a positive attitude:

I ran out of coffee at work so I tried a herbal tea instead and loved it/ got stuck in traffic because of the weather and instead of getting anxious about being late I kept calm and noticed a new cafe that looks perfect for a lazy brunch/ couldn't find my keys so emptied out my bag only to discover a discount voucher in there for my favourite pizza place that expires this week!

Today I performed these anonymous acts of kindness:

I brought a selection box of biscuits into the office for my colleagues to enjoy and left them in the kitchen when no one was watching/ left a book I really enjoyed in a local sandwich bar with a note for the person who finds it to enjoy and pass it on/ filled a bag with household items I no longer use that are in good shape and donated them to the local homeless shelter.

Today these were the moments when I stopped to 'smell the roses':

I surrendered to the fact that the traffic jam I was in was not out to get me and turned the radio up/ stopped looking at the computer when my partner called and instead gave them my full attention/ when I got home I sat for 5 full minutes in silence before switching on the distractions, like the TV and laptop.

#DAILYGRATITUDE

"Enjoyable times with family and friends. Warmth and love etc."

"Being born in this country and at this time in history. For no other reason than luck, I grew up in a peaceful country, with clean running water and with food on the table every day. That's got to be something to feel grateful for!"

"I used to live abroad and it was always hot and sunny. There was never a morning when I looked out of the window to see clouds or leaves falling. Of course, I was always grateful for that…but nothing beats the change in seasons, especially autumn. It gets me every time!"

"Choice! I am grateful for being able to make choices every day about how I live my life: where, with whom, how and so on. I know that not everyone has the choices I have because of their circumstances and that makes my independence even more valuable."

"At the moment, more than anything I am grateful for ancient wisdoms. I have been suffering from some fairly debilitating health issues and the remedies offered to me by my GP were not acceptable. Instead, I decided to try acupuncture and lo and behold the results have not only changed my life but they were fast. Amazing!"

"I am grateful for my gorgeous son."

DAY ONE

The first day of the rest of your life! Go for it!

Today I am grateful for:

Today I took these things for granted:

Today I experienced these difficulties that I can improve upon with a positive attitude:

Today I performed these anonymous acts of kindness:

Today these were the moments when I stopped to 'smell the roses':

#DAILYGRATITUDE

"I am grateful for the beautiful warm breeze that is wafting through my windows. It is a delight to see the fresh new leaves on our maple tree in front of our house flow in this breeze.

You get the gust of fresh air and the shimmer of the leaves in the sunlight and the whisper sound of the leaves as they flutter against each other. I am grateful for the Dyson that picks up all of the cat hair and scattered grains of pine. It works so well but the cats are none too pleased with me.

Had to pull out the dreaded Vaccuuuuuum today and had 3 frightened and one fascinated cat. Rollo was upstairs leaning through the rails to see what the heck that noise was all about. Ruthie and Johnny vanished in a flash as soon as I turned it on and Burke kept an eye on it from a distance for the whole time it was on. Scary stuff that vaccuuuuuuuum - but good for me.

I am very grateful that we were able to get it using Air Canada points from all of the traveling that my husband did over the years. For a long time he was away from the house all over the world on car junkets and he was gone at different intervals but if you add them all up I estimate it was more than 60 per cent of a year for at least 10 years.

So many destinations and I am very grateful that I got to share in quite a few of them. I have been blessed to see some fabulous locations around the world. And finally I am grateful that my husband has been able to fall asleep after being quite sick today.

I am grateful that I was here to help as much as a sympathetic vomiter can do. Another wonderful and wonder-filled day."

DAY TWO

Today I am grateful for:

Today I took these things for granted:

Today I experienced these difficulties that I can improve upon with a positive attitude:

Today I performed these anonymous acts of kindness:

Today these were the moments when I stopped to 'smell the roses':

#DAILYGRATITUDE

"I was diagnosed with Multiple Sclerosis years ago, and it has been taking its toll. BUT I can still walk and think clearly and do things.

My entire family has taken on the attitude of "If I can do something now, why wait for it? If I wait too long, I may not be able to do it!" I have been having many complicated health struggles, but I am HERE.

I am MARRIED. I am STILL WALKING. So I will work from my computer when I can, even though I can't stand for long periods of time anymore!"

DAY THREE

Today I am grateful for:

Today I took these things for granted:

Today I experienced these difficulties that I can improve upon with a positive attitude:

Today I performed these anonymous acts of kindness:

Today these were the moments when I stopped to 'smell the roses:'

#DAILYGRATITUDE

"Just being."

DAY FOUR

Today I am grateful for:

Today I took these things for granted:

Today I experienced these difficulties that I can improve upon with a positive attitude:

Today I performed these anonymous acts of kindness:

Today these were the moments when I stopped to 'smell the roses':

#DAILYGRATITUDE

"There are 12 sets of traffic lights between the motorway and my home. The day they were all green was a day of great joy!"

DAY FIVE

Today I am grateful for:

Today I took these things for granted:

Today I experienced these difficulties that I can improve upon with a positive attitude:

Today I performed these anonymous acts of kindness:

Today these were the moments when I stopped to 'smell the roses:'

#DAILYGRATITUDE

"I am grateful for my health, my friends, my husband, my life. I am grateful for having an inquisitive mind and I am grateful that I have an ability to put myself in others' shoes, my happiness comes from doing things for others."

DAY SIX

Today I am grateful for:

Today I took these things for granted:

Today I experienced these difficulties that I can improve upon with a positive attitude:

Today I performed these anonymous acts of kindness:

Today these were the moments when I stopped to 'smell the roses':

#DAILYGRATITUDE

"I'm most grateful for this life, this time on earth."

DAY SEVEN

Well done! Your first attitude to gratitude week is completed!
Today I am grateful for:

Today I took these things for granted:

Today I experienced these difficulties that I can improve upon with a positive attitude:

Today I performed these anonymous acts of kindness:

Today these were the moments when I stopped to 'smell the roses:'

#DAILYGRATITUDE

"Fab friends, kind and intelligent children and loving family/relationships, a job I enjoy that also pays the bills, good mental and physical health, a gin and tonic at the end of a long day, baked Camembert AND A MILLION OTHERS THINGS!"

DAY EIGHT

Today I am grateful for:

Today I took these things for granted:

Today I experienced these difficulties that I can improve upon with a positive attitude:

Today I performed these anonymous acts of kindness:

Today these were the moments when I stopped to 'smell the roses':

#DAILYGRATITUDE

"My incredible family, my health, my home, my fur babies, my potential and my dashing good looks ;) "

DAY NINE

Today I am grateful for:

Today I took these things for granted:

Today I experienced these difficulties that I can improve upon with a positive attitude:

Today I performed these anonymous acts of kindness:

Today these were the moments when I stopped to 'smell the roses:'

#DAILYGRATITUDE

"My family, job opportunities, my animals/pets, and my ability to remain positive despite challenging life events."

DAY TEN

Today I am grateful for:

Today I took these things for granted:

Today I experienced these difficulties that I can improve upon with a positive attitude:

Today I performed these anonymous acts of kindness:

Today these were the moments when I stopped to 'smell the roses':

#DAILYGRATITUDE

"My life, my body, my family, my partner, friends, nature and my good fortune. My parents and Kinny for looking after me, buying food online, the people who help me: Jurate, Teresa, Ariella. The therapists I see, particularly Anna A, Miguel M, Adrianna, Elizabeth A."

DAY ELEVEN

Today I am grateful for:

Today I took these things for granted:

Today I experienced these difficulties that I can improve upon with a positive attitude:

Today I performed these anonymous acts of kindness:

Today these were the moments when I stopped to 'smell the roses:'

#DAILYGRATITUDE

"Family (in particular my partner), friends in person and friends online, our cats and their calm approach to life, our home, my church and the fellowship with the women there, in our deanery and in our diocese, the change of seasons here in this beautiful country of Canada, nature all around us."

DAY TWELVE

Today I am grateful for:

Today I took these things for granted:

Today I experienced these difficulties that I can improve upon with a positive attitude:

Today I performed these anonymous acts of kindness:

Today these were the moments when I stopped to 'smell the roses':

#DAILYGRATITUDE

"I am MOST grateful for my family. Other relationships may come and go, but my family will always be. No matter how far apart from each other we are, we're still family, and we still keep in touch. We are always there for each other!"

DAY THIRTEEN

Today I am grateful for:

Today I took these things for granted:

Today I experienced these difficulties that I can improve upon with a positive attitude:

Today I performed these anonymous acts of kindness:

Today these were the moments when I stopped to 'smell the roses:'

#DAILYGRATITUDE

"Eternal salvation, the knowledge that eternity is more than this physical lifetime (an eternal perspective), and all the usual things: a home (I live in a castle right now), an intact marriage and multi-generational family, good health, a sound local church, the knowledge that most of my family are believers and that the others will become believers eventually, the beauty of the physical world and the opportunities I have because of God's daily provision."

DAY FOURTEEN

Good job! Your second attitude of gratitude week completed!

Today I am grateful for:

Today I took these things for granted:

Today I experienced these difficulties that I can improve upon with a positive attitude:

Today I performed these anonymous acts of kindness:

Today these were the moments when I stopped to 'smell the roses:'

#DAILYGRATITUDE

"I am grateful for my health, my friends, my husband, my life. I am grateful for having an inquisitive mind, and I am grateful that I have an ability to put myself in others shoes, my happiness comes from doing things for others."

DAY FIFTEEN

Today I am grateful for:

Today I took these things for granted:

Today I experienced these difficulties that I can improve upon with a positive attitude:

Today I performed these anonymous acts of kindness:

Today these were the moments when I stopped to 'smell the roses':

#DAILYGRATITUDE

"Family, friends, job."

DAY SIXTEEN

Celebrate!! Half your challenge is done! Today I am grateful for:

Today I took these things for granted:

Today I experienced these difficulties that I can improve upon with a positive attitude:

Today I performed these anonymous acts of kindness:

Today these were the moments when I stopped to 'smell the roses:'

#DAILYGRATITUDE

"My husband. He is my friend, my rock, my true companion and my human calculator."

DAY SEVENTEEN

Today I am grateful for:

Today I took these things for granted:

Today I experienced these difficulties that I can improve upon with a positive attitude:

Today I performed these anonymous acts of kindness:

Today these were the moments when I stopped to 'smell the roses':

#DAILYGRATITUDE

"My health, being alive, my children, my partner, family, friends and people who bring joy to my life. Being able to see and acknowledge joy, even in small amounts. Facing my own mortality was a massive, all-changing experience. I'm grateful for every single day. And medics!"

DAY EIGHTEEN

Today I am grateful for:

Today I took these things for granted:

Today I experienced these difficulties that I can improve upon with a positive attitude:

Today I performed these anonymous acts of kindness:

Today these were the moments when I stopped to 'smell the roses:'

#DAILYGRATITUDE

"For knowledge."

DAY NINETEEN

Today I am grateful for:

Today I took these things for granted:

Today I experienced these difficulties that I can improve upon with a positive attitude:

Today I performed these anonymous acts of kindness:

Today these were the moments when I stopped to 'smell the roses':

#DAILYGRATITUDE

"I love to be in love. I love to be loved. I love so many things: from people and things to feelings and experiences. I love to feel the wind against my skin as we drive along the coastal road. I love to listen to music and sing along loudly and out of tune. I love to be in silence. I love that I am able to love everything. Loving makes me feel truly alive. I am so grateful to be alive."

DAY TWENTY

Today I am grateful for:

Today I took these things for granted:

Today I experienced these difficulties that I can improve upon with a positive attitude:

Today I performed these anonymous acts of kindness:

Today these were the moments when I stopped to 'smell the roses:'

#DAILYGRATITUDE

"I'm grateful for easy communication. It's hard to imagine that years ago it took months for letters to travel from one country to another.

Imagine the hardships that the Pilgrims faced when they set up home in America. If they wanted to let their families know that they had arrived safely, or a baby had been born, or someone had passed away, the process of communicating with those most important to them was time-consuming and difficult. Now we have access to one another 24 hours a day.

Calling, texting, emailing, or even driving or traveling to visit someone is fast. We can always reach out and be connected with another human being within moments. Perhaps it doesn't always feel like we have constant access to others but we do."

DAY TWENTY-ONE

Well done! Three attitude to gratitude weeks down! Today I am grateful for:

Today I took these things for granted:

Today I experienced these difficulties that I can improve upon with a positive attitude:

Today I performed these anonymous acts of kindness:

Today these were the moments when I stopped to 'smell the roses:'

#DAILYGRATITUDE

"Learning from mistakes."

DAY TWENTY-TWO

Today I am grateful for:

Today I took these things for granted:

Today I experienced these difficulties that I can improve upon with a positive attitude:

Today I performed these anonymous acts of kindness:

Today these were the moments when I stopped to 'smell the roses:'

#DAILYGRATITUDE

"When friends from out of town come to visit and we learn to see our 'boring' and familiar surroundings through new eyes. It always reminds me that my city is full of amazing parks, museums, theatre shows and so on."

DAY TWENTY-THREE

Today I am grateful for:

Today I took these things for granted:

Today I experienced these difficulties that I can improve upon with a positive attitude:

Today I performed these anonymous acts of kindness:

Today these were the moments when I stopped to 'smell the roses':

#DAILYGRATITUDE

"Too much time is wasted comparing ourselves to others and wishing to be someone or something that we aren't; the cult of celebrity that we are fed daily by the media. Each of us has our own strengths and weaknesses and it's only when we accept everything that we are and that we are not, that we will truly find the happiness and fulfillment that we seek. I am grateful for being me."

DAY TWENTY-FOUR

Today I am grateful for:

Today I took these things for granted:

Today I experienced these difficulties that I can improve upon with a positive attitude:

Today I performed these anonymous acts of kindness:

Today these were the moments when I stopped to 'smell the roses:'

#DAILYGRATITUDE

"My parents for giving me life. Without them, there would be no me."

DAY TWENTY-FIVE

Today I am grateful for:

Today I took these things for granted:

Today I experienced these difficulties that I can improve upon with a positive attitude:

Today I performed these anonymous acts of kindness:

Today these were the moments when I stopped to 'smell the roses':

#DAILYGRATITUDE

"Today's gratitude is for what we have (and more often than not in amounts far greater than I ever give credit for), starting with life and life force. Having heard this morning of the sudden and unexpected death of someone we knew through friends, there's no time to sit around faffing and moaning.

Grab what you can out of life and make sure that each moment counts, whether that's following your dreams (seriously, what's the worst that can happen?), or just dreaming. Being thankful for the love that is shown to us each and every day - there's plenty of it to go round - by returning it. You and those you love deserve it.

Finally, I am grateful for the separated shoulder I currently have - it reminds me that if that is as bad as it gets right now, I am one very fortunate woman."

DAY TWENTY-SIX

Today I am grateful for:

Today I took these things for granted:

Today I experienced these difficulties that I can improve upon with a positive attitude:

Today I performed these anonymous acts of kindness:

Today these were the moments when I stopped to 'smell the roses:'

#DAILYGRATITUDE

"Well, so far it's a very good day and one to be thankful for. The footage from the shoot I did yesterday is superb and the client is happy - so I am very grateful for that. Our shipping boxes from the UK are being delivered today - very grateful that they got here at all even if it wasn't within the specified time limit, as we have survived without whatever is in them and have totally forgotten what we thought was so urgent that we would have to ship it. I am also extremely thankful for the blender we bought with free points from Sears as I am going to make a smoothie (banana, almond butter, mango, pineapple, kale and wheatgrass with coconut milk) in a moment!"

"Feeling like a child again by lying on the ground and watching the clouds or the stars."

DAY TWENTY-SEVEN

Today I am grateful for:

Today I took these things for granted:

Today I experienced these difficulties that I can improve upon with a positive attitude:

Today I performed these anonymous acts of kindness:

Today these were the moments when I stopped to 'smell the roses':

#DAILYGRATITUDE

"For the not knowing."

DAY TWENTY-EIGHT

Woohoo! Just three more days to go! Today I am grateful for:

Today I took these things for granted:

Today I experienced these difficulties that I can improve upon with a positive attitude:

Today I performed these anonymous acts of kindness:

Today these were the moments when I stopped to 'smell the roses:'

#DAILYGRATITUDE

"Waking up and seeing a bright blue sky when you look out of the window for the first time in the morning."

DAY TWENTY-NINE

Wow! You are almost there! Today I am grateful for:

Today I took these things for granted:

Today I experienced these difficulties that I can improve upon with a positive attitude:

Today I performed these anonymous acts of kindness:

Today these were the moments when I stopped to 'smell the roses':

#DAILYGRATITUDE

"For beginnings and endings."

DAY THIRTY

You've done it! Congratulations! Today I am grateful for:

Today I took these things for granted:

Today I experienced these difficulties that I can improve upon with a positive attitude:

Today I performed these anonymous acts of kindness:

Today these were the moments when I stopped to 'smell the roses:'

#DAILYGRATITUDE

"For everything."

WELL DONE!

You have done it! 30 days of **#dailygratitude** completed and numerous acts of kindness enacted by you. You have single-handedly made this world a better place for yourself and for others. Hopefully, you have enjoyed this journey and noticed a positive difference in your own life and will continue to have an #attitudeofgratitude going forward - during the good times and the difficulties, too.

Namaste.

BONUS AFFIRMATIONS!

After all of your hard work over the past 30 days, you didn't think I would just leave you stranded without something to take forward and help you maintain and build on all that you have achieved? What kind of person do you think I am?

I truly want you to live your absolute best life, be the happiest and most successful person you can be and achieve things that you haven't yet even dreamed of. The best way to do that is to believe in yourself. Believing in ourselves is often the hardest thing of all to master but it is entirely possible.

We all have our own stories and obstacles that we have to 'get over' and it's not as simple as just willing those things into oblivion, or ignoring them. Accepting and loving ourselves for who we are including all of the 'stuff,' is the most powerful and loving thing each of us can do for ourselves and for the world, regardless of how difficult or uncomfortable those things make us feel.

From this moment forwards be kind to yourself and know that each day is a brand new opportunity to create your best life.

"How?!" I hear you cry.

Well, it's simple: affirmations.

What on earth is an affirmation and how is that going to help me do anything? An affirmation is a simple positive statement that you repeat to yourself.

In much the same way as lifting weights every day, however small, will eventually improve your muscle tone, repeating affirmations daily will improve your mind (both consciously and subconsciously).

Repeating these positive mantras to yourself daily will help you to overcome those negative thoughts and limiting beliefs that pop up when you least want them to. For me they are loudest when something good is about to happen and fill me with dread and self doubt. Or they did before 'affirmations.'

Many successful people know this simple method of 'programming' their brains to enable them to achieve their aims and many popular books have been published on the subject.

You don't even have to believe that these affirmations will work for you - you just have to follow the instructions below and give them a few moments of your time. Before you know it your life will have the 'muscles' needed to make it work better and more powerfully for you.

Supplies required:

- ◊ Willingness to give affirmations a go
- ◊ An empty jar with a lid
- ◊ A pair of scissors.

On the following pages are thirty affirmations for you to cut out and keep. Fold each of them neatly and place in the jar. Each morning give the jar a little shake, pick one and say it out loud. Perhaps you can take a snapshot of it using your mobile phone, or write it down so it is with you and repeat the affirmation throughout the day.

Replace the affirmation back in the jar and repeat every day. If you pick out the same affirmation on consecutive days, it might be that the Universe is letting you know that this particular message is important to you and needs more work.

Most of all - enjoy the process - and good luck!

I accept myself fully and gratefully and thrive each and every day in peacefulness.

I actively see the best in everything and it brings the best to me.

I congratulate myself for all I have achieved and achieve all that I have dreamed of.

I believe in my value to the world and the world values me.

I calmly forgive myself for the mistakes I have made and know that they propel me forwards in life.

I celebrate my life and create more wonderful things to celebrate.

I congratulate myself for being kind to myself and others and am deeply loved in return.

I courageously accept all that I am and am filled with confidence and joy.

I delight in the world around me and the world responds by offering me more each day.

I effectively complete tasks and fill my life with achievements.

I progress towards my goals and live a life I had only ever dreamed of.

I energise myself with a brisk walk, or dance like no one is watching and feel good all day.

I enthusiastically face the day and all of the wonderful things it brings me in return.

I easily achieve my goals and attract more rewards each day.

I give myself permission to breathe fully and deeply and to absorb the Universe's blessings.

I grow something from seed and celebrate the wonder of life by creating more positivity, success and wealth.

I gladly face the day because it is filled with love, happiness, good health, wealth and safety.

I hug at least one person each day and make a connection that empowers me and boosts my immunity.

I imagine what is positive and possible and make all of my dreams come true.

I learn something new; perhaps a poem, a recipe, a foreign word and it enhances my life and opportunities.

I marvel at my achievements and am inspired to achieve bigger and better in all areas of my life.

I mean what I say and am filled with the confidence to do as I say and improve myself and my circumstances.

I joyfully choose nutritious food, drink and lifestyle and am the healthiest I have ever been and more energised.

I open my heart to all that is good in the world and the world responds by giving me more to be thankful for.

I optimistically live my life and attract amazing people, opportunities and adventures.

I smile at the world and the world bestows riches upon me.

I trust my decisions and am rewarded with untold benefits.

I value my time and my days are filled with amazing experiences and people.

I welcome wealth in all of its forms and am grateful to have enough of everything.

I say yes to all opportunities that I am blessed with and am living my best life.

SOCIALISE WITH US!

FaceBook:
www.facebook.com/
AttitudeofGratitudeBooks/

Website:
www.100percentpublishing.com

JOIN OUR SURVEY

info@100percentpublishing.com

Printed in Great Britain
by Amazon

54661697R00127